D1459192

APOCKETFUL
OFHOUSES

Edited by Robyn Beaver

APOCKETFUL OFHOUSES

images
Publishing

First reprinted in 2007
(The Images Publishing Group Reference Number: 735)

Published in Australia in 2006 by
The Images Publishing Group Pty Ltd
ABN 89 059 734 431
6 Bastow Place, Mulgrave, Victoria 3170, Australia
Tel: +61 3 9561 5544 Fax: +61 3 9561 4860
books@images.com.au
www.imagespublishing.com

National Library of Australia Cataloguing-in-Publication entry:

A pocketful of houses.

Includes index.
ISBN 978 1 86470 189 0.

1. Architecture, Domestic – Pictorial works.

728

Edited by Robyn Beaver

Designed by The Graphic Image Studio Pty Ltd, Mulgrave, Australia
www.tgis.com.au

Digital production by Splitting Image Colour Studio Pty Ltd, Australia
Printed by Everbest Printing Co. Ltd. in Hong Kong/China

IMAGES has included on its website a page for special notices
in relation to this and its other publications. Please visit www.imagespublishing.com

Contents

Contents

PROJECTS

222 Residence

Oklahoma, USA
Elliott + Associates Architects

The owner was able to convince the developer to allow the construction of a "modern" house in a proposed "traditional" neighborhood. The conditions were that the modern house had to be invisible from the street and that the design would have to be approved by the local architectural review committee.

The architectural aim was to create a house that emerges from the earth, blending the site, soil, place, and form into an expression inspired by the unique conditions of this place and time.

The client's program wishes for the 3500-square-foot (325-square-meter) residence were detailed and precise. Included were requests for a "safe room" and sauna, an office for two people, a kitchen to accommodate a professional chef, exercise room, an outdoor living room, a lap pool, and a saltwater aquarium. Access into the house for the two family dogs was also mandatory.

Approach to the house begins with a curving, naturally landscaped entry road with a security "art" gate for monitored access to the house. A freestanding concrete wall with moveable, colored acrylic rods provides an ever-changing interactive arrival point at the front door. This, along with a 20 x 9-foot (6 x 3-meter) yellow steel frame, extends and captures visual fragments beyond the glass, blurring the distinction between indoors and outdoors.

The linear plan separates, and puts in sequence, public and private spaces with narrow glass connector spaces stitching them together. The spaces are created to provide unique personal moments in time, such as the view of a unique landscape feature from the bathtub or watching the wildlife from an exposed glass shower.

The interior finishes include a stained concrete slab the color of the soil, as if the site moves through the structure. Spatial warmth is created with surface and color. Above the kitchen counter is a glowing opening acting as art, and a man-made reminder of the seasons. Glass acts as an invisible separation to the natural world beyond, regardless of whether it is the shower, toilet, tub or kitchen. The glass garden on the north provides an unexpected pocket-sized Zen garden fashioned from recycled glass.

Photography: Hedrich Blessing

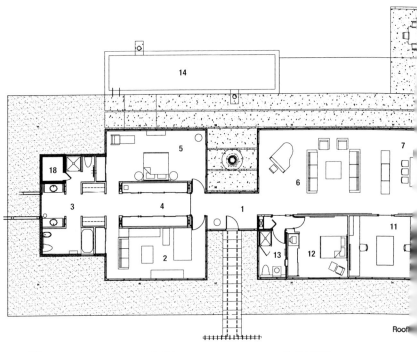

1 Main entry	7 Dining	13 Guest bath
2 Exercise room	8 Kitchen	14 Lap pool
3 Master bathroom	9 Garage	15 Patio with outdoor fireplace
4 Master dressing room	10 Utility room	16 Dog entrance
5 Master bedroom	11 Office	17 Glass garden
6 Living room	12 Guest bedroom	18 Sauna/safe room

Roof

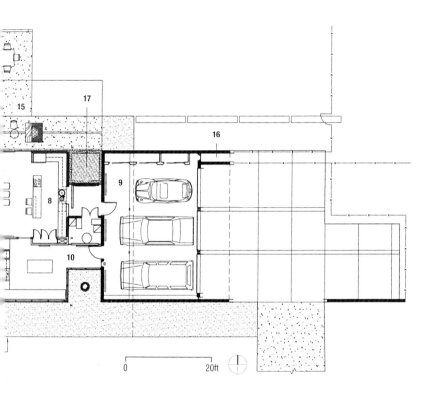

15

16

17

9

8

10

0   20ft

511 House

Pacific Palisades, California, USA
Kanner Architects

The challenge in the design of the 511 House was to create a bright, modern, Southern California home able to embrace the outdoors. Blurring the line between inside and outside was of the highest priority. To do this, the main body of the two-story plan was pushed to the north side of the standard tennis court-sized lot. A wide patio extends to the south off the lower level and it is this generous setback that enables the southern light to penetrate the house. Large sliding glass doors pull away, allowing the inside to merge with the outside.

The modernist esthetic is inspired by nearby houses by Richard Neutra and Charles and Ray Eames. However, it is a house of its time and is completely unique as its textures, materials and fenestrations make a personal statement. There is a metaphorical juxtaposition of rough to smooth materials (scratch-coat plaster versus smooth mosaic tile) that recalls the relationship of the ocean to the mountains. Landscaping is critical to the scheme as it is the key to creating a private world. Timber bamboo, black bamboo, and ficus hedges are placed in front of horizontally slatted cedar fencing, screening neighboring homes. Gravel paths at the drip line and a large lawn surround to the south and west. At the street, a V-shaped specimen palm layers the front façade, while bands of Japanese grass, gravel and lawn graphically recall the scoring pattern in the front yard hardscape.

The 511 House is about Southern California living—inside/out. The plan, section and site plan are of greatest importance. How can a typical lot be utilized to make it seem larger and more open? Solving the planning problems in a unique way allows the design of the envelope to become secondary. This is a house about lifestyle, not just another home with a contemporary façade.

Photography: John Linden Photographer

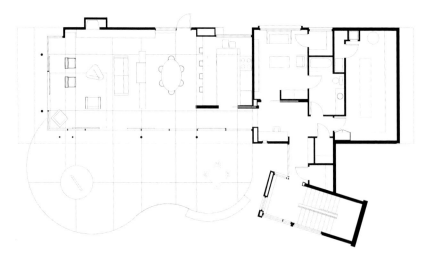

700 Palms Residence

Venice, California, USA
Steven Ehrlich Architects

This residence was designed as a flexible compound for large family gatherings and overnight guests. Key requirements were to maximize volume, light and privacy on a narrow urban lot, and employ sustainability and sensitivity to scale and context. Built of raw, honest materials appropriate to the bohemian grittiness of Venice, the house dissolves the barriers between indoors and out, creating multi-use spaces that fully exploit the benign climate.

The site is a 43 x 132-foot (13 x 40-meter) lot on the corner of a street of traditional beach bungalows, lined with palms. At two stories plus a mezzanine level, the house, as well as its separate garage/guest house, is taller than most of its neighbors. The mass has been peeled back and mitigated on the upper levels by two large sheltering pine trees and a palm, one of which graces each of three distinct courtyards. Walls and landscaping screen the two street façades.

The wood-and-steel frame structure is outlined by a steel exoskeleton, from which automatic light scrims roll down to shield the front façade from the western sun. The 16-foot-high (5-meter) living/dining area opens up on three sides: to the lap pool on the west with sliding glass doors; to the north courtyard and guest house with pocketing glass doors; and to the garden to the south through pivoting metal doors. When opened entirely to the elements, the structure is an airy

pavilion, with temperate ocean breezes making air-conditioning unnecessary. The concrete slab absorbs the sun's warmth in the winter and has a radiant heat source for cold nights, and photovoltaic panels at the roofline store and augment energy.

Shifts from confined to lofty spaces animate the design. Space is compressed at the low front entrance of the house, and then explodes into the main volume. Stairs lead up to a pair of mezzanine-level sleeping/lounging lofts with decks; a glass bridge spans the living room and leads to another flight of stairs up to the master bedroom and study. The top floor is flooded with light from a shed roof that opens a long clerestory to the western sky.

Rough and smooth surfaces contrast throughout the house. The western front façade, a clearly defined mass, is clad inside and out in Corten steel. Ample metal overhangs and fascias are of metal and parklex. The interior back wall of shot-blasted structural concrete masonry is a backdrop for artwork.

Photography: Erhard Pfeiffer, Julius Shulman & Juergen Nogai

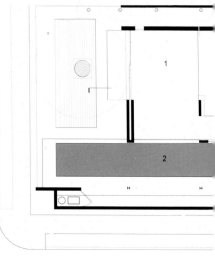

1 Living space
2 Pool
3 Entry
4 Powder room
5 Dining room
6 Kitchen
7 Laundry
8 Storage
9 Garage

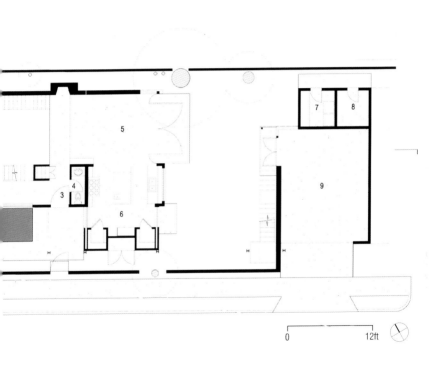

A House in the Country

Aconcagua Valley, Chile
Germán del Sol, Architect

This large family country home in the Aconcagua Valley, Chile, was built on a 70-acre (28-hectare) grassland site. The floor level of the house is raised 5 feet (1.5 meters) above the ground to capture sunlight and distant views, while retaining the privacy of the patios, the big open spaces associated with country life. Rough, low-maintenance materials have been used throughout the indoor and outdoor living areas to provide maximum comfort. A dispersed and crisscrossed floor plan extends the façade's length and forms long, shaded terraces around the house. Rooms have been designed with flexibility in mind, allowing for changes in use as the family's needs change.

Photography Guy St. Clare

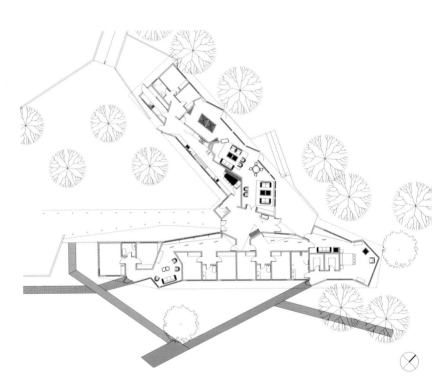

Atlanta Residence

Atlanta, Georgia, USA
Olson Sundberg Kundig Allen Architects

This new house in an historic Atlanta neighborhood uses modern materials to express the mystique of the old South. Traditional elements found in historic Southern mansions—front columns, a portico, Palladian spatial arrangement, and an emphasis on the staircase—were reinterpreted to subtly connect the house to the region's strong architectural heritage. Space flows freely from inside to outside, and vistas amplify the sense of space on this relatively narrow urban lot.

Photography: Scott Jenks, Bruce Van Inwegen

Bangkok House

Bangkok, Thailand
Jackson Clements Burrows Architects
HASSELL Limited, Thailand

This 7532-square-foot (700-square-meter), two-story residence is located in central Bangkok, Thailand. The brief was to design a substantial family house that would offer withdrawal and sanctuary from the hectic nature of the surrounding city.

The site is located within a gated residential precinct with adjacent buildings presenting their backs to the site—an unimpressive collage of balconies, downpipes, air-conditioning condensers, water tanks and clothes lines. This condition provided an opportunity to explore a courtyard house typology, in this case, two linear forms shield the primary outdoor space.

Entry is through a double-height breezeway that connects the two forms. This space opens on axis to the swimming pool and courtyard garden beyond. Here a choice is made to proceed into either of two wings: to the left the informal living area surrounds a functional kitchen and scullery with a generous adjoining study; a master bedroom suite and guest bedroom suite are located above on the first floor. To the right is a formal lounge and entertaining area serviced by a bar. The first floor accommodates the children's bedrooms, study, and rumpus areas. Service spaces, housing housekeeper's quarters, a double garage, laundry and steam room for the pool, discreetly adjoin both wings.

This house attempts to embrace the tropical climate through provision of various private outdoor retreat spaces. The key zone uniting the house is the courtyard garden, which benefits from shade and offers a comfortable outdoor seating space. This space links the two ground-floor living areas and informal meals often occur in this location. The seating area is protected by a floating roof that provides filtered shade and allows use during frequent rain. Upstairs, the primary bedrooms also address protected decks with elevated garden views—private retreat spaces which can be occupied individually. The house can be cross-ventilated in two directions, minimizing the need for air conditioning when possible. This cooling process is assisted by openable doors and windows located adjacent to the pool. The house often remains completely open to the courtyard, blurring the distinction between inside and out.

This house, through its interpretation of the courtyard typology, offers a unique variation on Asian central city life. Separation is provided by independent retreat spaces, but unity is achieved in the central courtyard space which draws the occupants to its subconscious microclimate—a unique sense of place which seems to remove any awareness of the city beyond.

Photography: John Gollings, Gollings Photography Pty Ltd

Belvedere Residence

Belvedere, California, USA
CCS Architecture

Located right along the Bay, this project is a total and complete renovation of a two-story residence—the primary home for a family of five—and includes the development of the entire site from fence to fence and from street to water.

The dramatic setting and orientation of the site drove the design for this project. Starting from the street, an axis leads to the house, pierces it as a two-story central hall, and continues to the bay as a dock, aligning with Mt Tamalpias across the water. This 'through-axis' organization creates strong spatial connections to the water on the north and to the landscape of the site on the south. This also results in an enlargement of the overall perception, which posits the dichotomy of land versus water. This same organization occurs in two parallel ways—where flanking the central hall are living and dining on one side, kitchen and family on the other—both with equal width openings at opposite ends which establish the connections to the landscape and the water.

The second floor consists of three bedrooms with panoramic views of Marin and the immediate landscape. The site's landscape is a combination of limestone paving, lawn, and contained planting. The existing mature olive trees were relocated throughout as elements of scale, balance, and Mediterranean reference. The interior is a restrained palette of crisp white walls playing off limestone floors, natural wood, and steel.

Photography: Cesar Rubio

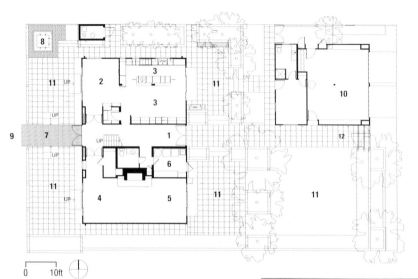

1 Entry
2 Family room
3 Kitchen/breakfast
4 Dining room
5 Living room
6 Utility room
7 Deck/dock
8 Jacuzzi
9 San Francisco Bay
10 Garage/guest
11 Site landscape
12 Entry/gate

0   10ft

Bernal Heights Residence

San Francisco, California, USA
CCS Architecture

This remodel of an existing three-story house transforms the interior with an airy, free-flowing space for living that opens to sweeping southern views of San Francisco.

The house was streamlined into three distinct and rejuvenated tiers for different aspects of the client's life. The ground floor work focused on entry improvements and a garage structural upgrade to accommodate the client's collection of vintage cars. The third floor was renovated as the most private part of the house, offering a master bedroom and two guest bedrooms to be grown into as the client looks forward to a future family. Between the two is the second floor—a new focal point of living, cooking, dining. This space—the center of most of the work—opens up the house's full floor area to daylight and southern views over San Francisco. Nearly all walls were removed and the floor was reorganized as a single contiguous space, half of which gathers at a monolithic, minimal kitchen-island. The client loves to cook and eat with friends; the new second floor responds with generous space for informal entertaining while cooking, as well as a stretch of dining area along the length of the house.

Here, the southern exterior wall has been stripped open by a ribbon of windows and a glass door that will provide access to a future deck over the backyard. By contrast, the north wall of the floor is lined with an understated but playful grid of shelves for books, artifacts from the client's travels, a stereo system, and liquor.

The second floor forms a center for the house, both a place to gather and to be sent back out to the city. It also contains many functions for living—both present and future—within a space that feels essentially open, airy, and uncluttered.

Photography: Eric Laignel

THE PRE-WAR SURFING
PHOTOGRAPHS OF DON JAMES
JULY 1 TO AUGUST 14, 1999
DANZIGER GALLERY
851 MADISON AVENUE
NEW YORK 10021

Berry House

Atlanta, Georgia, USA
William T. Baker & Associates

The Berry House is located in Druid Hills, a historic Atlanta neighborhood originally laid out by Frederick Law Olmstead, one of America's greatest landscape architects. The neighborhood's focal points are its Olmstead chain of parks bordered by wide tree-lined streets and the Druid Hill Golf Club. The Berry House is located on a quiet street that adjoins the golf course with park views at the front, and views of the golf course fairways at the rear.

The clients wanted their house to blend in with those surrounding it, especially the English-style homes from the 1920s. They had originally planned to purchase an original home but when they could not find one to suit their needs, decided that building a new "old" house was the best approach. The clients knew they had achieved that goal when a passerby asked how long it had taken to renovate this old house.

The two-story house features hand-carved limestone, a heavy variegated slate roof, and old-world brick. Superb interior detailing completes its authenticity.

Photography: James Lockheart, Stone Mountain, Georgia

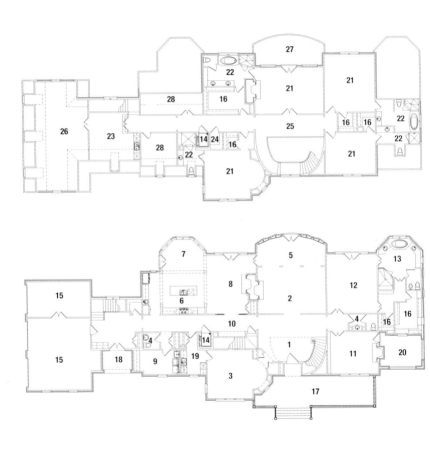

1 Foyer
2 Living room
3 Dining room
4 Powder room
5 Sun room
6 Kitchen
7 Breakfast
8 Family room
9 Laundry room
10 Gallery
11 Library
12 Master suite
13 Master bathroom
14 Elevator
15 Garage
16 Closet
17 Front terrace
18 Service entrance
19 Butler's pantry
20 Covered porch
21 Bedroom
22 Bathroom
23 Media room
24 Linen
25 Upper hall
26 Exercise room
27 Open terrace
28 Storage

Berty House

East Hampton, New York, USA
Alfredo De Vido Associates

The clients wanted a house for either weekend or full-time use in an exurban area. They both admired the vernacular architecture of the area and so the resulting building used wood as its main building material. The approach to the house is marked by a series of pools and a kinetic sculpture designed by the architect. The landscape around the building is handsome and features a number of gardens planned by the owners. Bridges provide points of entry to the house over the gardens.

As the owners enjoy entertaining, the main floor contains a space large enough to hold 100 for a sit-down dinner. A fireplace is the focal point of one end of the room and at the other there is an 'art wall' to hold changing displays of paintings and sculpture. Lighting is built in and has the capability of varying its levels.

The main downstairs space is a media center and family room. Off this space is a workroom which is accessible to a greenhouse above. The greenhouse is another sitting area, which is mainly built of glass, is sunny, and filled with plants. This room can also be reached from the living room via a bridge. Nearby are decks with trellis, pleasant for outdoor dining in fine weather and close to the vegetable

and flower gardens. Overhangs and brise soleil regulate the strong summer sun while admitting beneficial winter sun to the building. An important consideration in the planning was thermal efficiency and syphonic cooling which is provided for with high, operable skylights and low intakes.

Photography: Norman McGrath

Bordeaux House

Bordeaux, France
Rem Koolhaas, Office of Metropolitan Architecture

This house was specifically designed to accommodate a wheelchair-bound husband and his wife. The couple purchased land on a mountain with panoramic city views, and instructed the architect to design a complex house rather than a simple house to define the husband's world.

The architect designed a house that is really three houses on top of each other. The lowest is a series of caverns carved from a hill for intimate family life. The highest level is divided into an area for the couple and one for their children. The most important level is a glass room sandwiched in the middle—half inside and half outside—which is almost invisible.

The husband has his own room or station, with a 3x3.5-metre lift that moves between the three levels, changing the plan and function with each movement between the floors. A single wall next to the elevator intersects each floor and contains everything the husband might need—books, artwork, and wine from the cellar.

The elevator is the heart of the house with each movement changing the architecture.

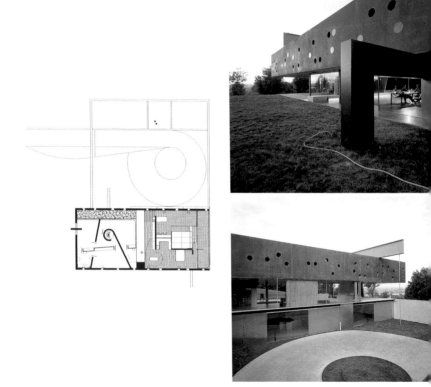

Brosmith Residence

Beverly Hills, California, USA
Zoltan E. Pali, FAIA; Studio Pali Fekete Architects (SPF:a)

The Brosmith Residence sensitively sites a single-family residence on a ridgeline of Mulholland Scenic Parkway, overlooking the San Fernando Valley of Southern California. In accordance with the client's objectives, the structure captures exterior space as living space, and harnesses the panoramic views of the valley below, accessible from the common areas and courtyards of the property. Separate living pods along a central spine of the 5000-square-foot (465-square-meter) house allow different activities and interactions to occur simultaneously without mutual disruption. Each living pod is outfitted with its own version of an indoor–outdoor courtyard space, and each is connected independently to the central spine of the house. Pods are designed around the master suite, the children's quarters, offices, and caretaker's quarters. Entering into the common living areas, one is met with breathtaking vistas of the San Fernando Valley, climaxing on the main patio where a glass-like swimming pool disappears entrancingly over the crisp clean horizon of the site's northern edge.

The energy-conserving structure uses passive siting and natural shading to reduce its dependence on mechanical environmental conditioning systems. Courtyards are located to take advantage of prevailing breezes. Innovative uses of standard materials create much of the custom feel of this residence, where concept and design elevates the feel of every room. A sliding louvered screen in the master suite uses an off-the-shelf, affordable aluminum frame (echoed elsewhere in the house) fitted with aluminum louvers substituted for glass, creating a unique application that seamlessly integrates with the clean lines of the house.

Photography: John Linden

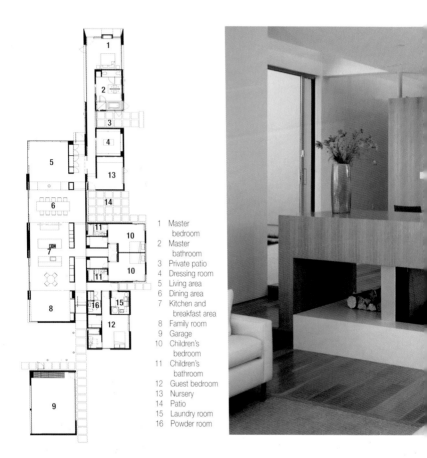

1 Master bedroom
2 Master bathroom
3 Private patio
4 Dressing room
5 Living area
6 Dining area
7 Kitchen and breakfast area
8 Family room
9 Garage
10 Children's bedroom
11 Children's bathroom
12 Guest bedroom
13 Nursery
14 Patio
15 Laundry room
16 Powder room

Casa Hachem

São Paulo, Brazil
Raul di Pace

The "Jardim America" neighborhood of São Paulo, where this house is located, was designed in 1913. It was then, and is today, a model of urban intervention, offering a high standard of living to the owners of the lots, with their standard "house plus garden" configuration. In earlier times, the houses had low walls and formed a harmonious whole with their eclectic architecture and front gardens.

In 1913 this was a peripheral zone of São Paulo; today it is located in the area known as "the espandid center," surrounded by dense traffic. Consequently, the façade characteristics and the main access to the houses have changed, to provide improved safety and privacy for the resident families. The first house built on this lot was smaller, and surrounded by a beautiful garden, which has survived till now despite all the changes made to the house over the years.

In 2003 the architect was engaged to design a new project on the site. The existing house was comfortable but divided into small rooms with very few spaces opening to the outside and the garden was not used to its full capacity.

The architect's idea was to return to the original reference, of the house surrounded by a garden, bringing light to the inside, and creating a transparent environment with an expansive view of the garden. To achieve these goals, the masonry walls were transformed into glass walls with a steel structure, creating the transparency required for the new context. The visual boundaries of the house were thus transferred to the outer edge of the site, amplifying the sensation of space and aiming to recover part of the original concept of the English house and garden.

Photography Courtesy Raul D. Pace

Connecticut Residence

Connecticut, USA
Elliott + Associates Architects

We had three conceptual goals. We wanted to create a house whose very existence is inspired by a modern and African art collection. It was to be a place where the interior and exterior embrace in appreciation of one another. It was our intent to appreciate classic modernism. There are no trends, no fashion, no tricks. At the outset, our intention was to enhance and develop the interior/exterior relationships. The 10-foot-high (3-meter) steel-and-glass curtain wall creates the envelope of the structure without imposing spatial boundaries. The relationship between man and nature is a 1-inch separation physically and zero visually. The window mullions become delicate picture frames outlining nature beyond. In this house, nature becomes art.

The structure is perched atop a hill overlooking an Atlantic Ocean tributary with natural stone outcroppings defining the perimeter and its wetlands. The glass wall along the northeast elevation provides a stunning view into the treetops creating the sensation of being suspended between the 70-foot-tall (21-meter) trees. This is a house where moods change by day and night; when the trees are green or bare or covered with snow or softened by fog. This house is a declaration of how beautiful man and nature can be in harmony. Modern architecture and nature are beautiful together.

The primary goal for the interior architecture is to create surroundings that complement and enhance the display of modern art and African sculpture. Special consideration was given to the African sculpture with the use of polished black granite slabs that visually absorb their bases and highlight the shapes with pure white backgrounds.

Awards include: American Institute of Architects, National Honor Award for Interiors; American Society of Interior Designers, National Interior Design Project Award.

Photography: Bob Shimer/Hedrich-Blessing

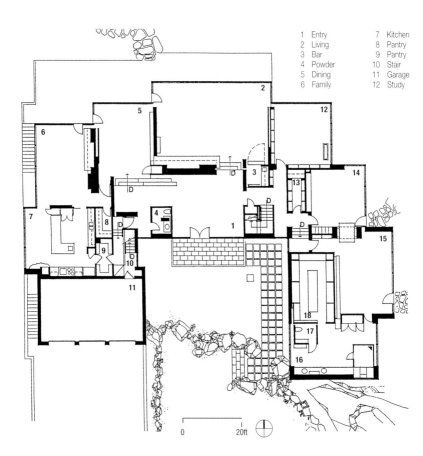

1	Entry	7	Kitchen
2	Living	8	Pantry
3	Bar	9	Pantry
4	Powder	10	Stair
5	Dining	11	Garage
6	Family	12	Study

0   20ft

Copper House

Massachusetts, USA
Charles Rose Architects Inc

The challenge of this renovation was to add a wing to an existing 1940's kit home. The original house was sited poorly on the south side of a 1-acre (0.4-hectare) hillside lot. An attached garage to the north obscured the spacious yard from the interior of the house. The garage was demolished and the addition was sited in its place. This siting preserved an east-facing terrace and created a west-facing entry court.

The design integrates and distinguishes between the old and new architectures. Formally, aesthetic dissonance is reduced by wrapping the original house in a monolithic, neutral cedar scrim; experientially, the historically inspired interior characteristics and small scale of the original structure are preserved.

The two-story addition is oriented east–west. The addition is opened to the site on the north, east, and west sides, and contains the main living spaces of the house, as well as the master bedroom and two offices on the second floor. A roof terrace with a hearth has panoramic views of the site and of Boston. A glass and steel stair connects the first and second floors, and an exterior stair leads to the roof deck from a deck off the master bedroom. A three-story skylit space mediates between the larger scale of the new and the smaller scale of the old, and serves as entry and circulation to the house.

Exterior construction materials include sheet copper, mahogany and Alaskan cedar windows, exposed aggregate concrete, painted steel, western red cedar siding, and bluestone. Interior materials include hardwood and bamboo floors, beech veneer paneling and casework, painted steel, and bluestone.

Photography: John Edward Linden

Coromandel Bach

Coromandel, New Zealand
Crosson Clarke Architects

The house was conceived as a container sitting lightly on the land for habitation or the dream of habitation. The intention was to reinterpret the New Zealand building tradition of the crafting of wood—the expression of structure, cladding, lining and joinery in a raw and unique way. The construction is reminiscent of the trip or rafter dams common in the Coromandel region at the turn of last century: heavy vertical structural members supporting horizontal boarding.

The unadorned natural timber, a sustainable and renewable resource, provides a connection to nature and the natural. A simple mechanism to the deck allows the box to open up on arrival, providing a stage for living, and to close down on departure, providing protection. The house has a simple, rectangular plan that sits across the contour in a patch of cleared bush in the manner of the rural shed, facing north and the view. The living room is open to the outside and the sun, a metaphorical tent or campsite, while the bunkrooms are enclosed and cool. The large fireplace allows winter occupation and the open bathroom and movable bath allows the rituals of showering and bathing to become an experience connected to nature.

This bach is an attempt to provide an environment to capture the essential spirit of the New Zealand holiday in the New Zealand landscape.

'Bach' is a typically New Zealand word that describes a weekend cottage or house, usually at the beach.

Photography: Patrick Reynolds

Crescent House

Wiltshire, UK
Dr Ken Shuttleworth, Architect

The house is modest and austere. Its simple form reacts strongly with the location, reflecting the various contrasts that the site offers as well as its historical context. The critical ingredients are a variety of spaces related to their function, a response to the changing quality of natural light, sensory contact with the elements of nature and the changing seasons, and a model for family living which is ecologically sensitive.

The concept is a series of simple, pure forms of white finished concrete and glass. Internally different types of space are created, related to the type of activity and varying quality of light. The normal clutter of architectural detail and designer items has been eliminated.

The design concept has two distinct, strongly contrasting sides. The northeast, which contains the private spaces, is adjacent to the other houses, the road, and poorer views. It presents a solid and translucent convex wall that increases privacy, reduces the effects of the westerly winds, and offers a robust, simple image to the approach. The southeast, with good views and exposure to the sun, is exactly the opposite—a concave crescent of clear glass reaches out to embrace the landscape and capture the views—offering maximum contact with nature from the living spaces. A double-height gallery and circulation are between the two crescents.

Photography: Nigel Young

Crescent Road House

Toronto, Ontario, Canada
Superkül Inc. Architect

With children grown up and with families of their own, the clients wanted to build a new home for themselves, tailored to the smaller scale of a two-person family.

Knowing they wanted to stay in the South Rosedale neighborhood they had been in for more than 30 years, but not able to find a suitable site on which to build, they severed their existing property. The resulting lot, measuring 44 x 138 feet (13.5 x 42.2 meters), contains an existing coach house at the rear and several mature trees.

The architect's intent was to design a modern townhouse that would comply with applicable setback and building height regulations and be a respectful intervention in the surrounding traditional fabric. To achieve this, materials and proportional relationships for the new house took their cues from neighboring houses. Red brick, dark wood siding, and bronze anodized window frames were used, the subdivision of the front façade and building massing respond to the adjacent houses, and a horizontal canopy defines the entrance forecourt addressing the gentle curve of the street.

The 2725-square-foot (250-square-meter) house has three principal volumes: two, two-story brick and wood boxes that contain and form a taller two-and-a-half story atrium in the center. The center atrium is the vertical and horizontal fulcrum of the design. It is the principal ordering element of the three main living spaces of the lower floor: kitchen/dining, atrium, and living room, and separates the different sleeping and study quarters of the upper floor. A glazed lantern tops the center atrium, bringing light deep into the middle of the house and providing for passive cooling and ventilation by convection with the use of motorized operable vents. An open stone staircase wraps around a lift that rises up the atrium leading to a mezzanine level overlooking the lower floor.

The existing coach house at the rear is restored and converted into a garage and hobby workshop space. An exterior court extends the interior space of the house to the outdoors. The wonderful 48-year-old magnolia tree at the front of the property, a well-recognized and highly appreciated tree in the community, especially when in bloom, remains.

Photography: Tom Arban

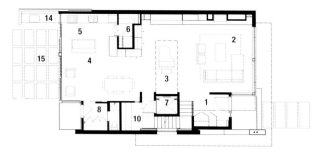

1 Front entry
2 Living
3 Atrium
4 Dining
5 Kitchen
6 Pantry/storage
7 Lift
8 Mud room
9 Open to below
10 Study/work desk
11 Bedroom
12 Dressing
13 Balcony
14 Built-in barbeque
15 Courtyard

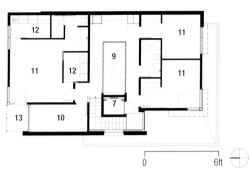

0   6ft

Dalwhinnie

Queenstown, New Zealand
Murray Cockburn Partnership

Set high above Lake Wakatipu, in the mountains of the South Island, this luxuriously proportioned residence provides the clients with some of New Zealand's most spectacular panoramic views. The site, bounded by sheer cliffs and steeply forested falls, is situated on a rounded rocky ridge, below Mt. Ben Lomond. Its aspect is primarily south, but the house has been purpose-built to capture all the magnificent vistas from the northeast around to the southwest, including The Remarkables, Cecil Peak, Walter Peak, and the Von Valley.

The unusual design concept uses a three-level configuration, and embraces a primary circle comprising two half-circles, one smaller than the other. A central drum tower, enclosing a thick-stepped, timber spiral staircase, made from native Rimu, locks the house into the bedrock. The tower is the pivotal point for the great, cantilevered steel I-beams, which support the upper two levels of the house and the wide, sweeping, mid-level balcony. The smaller, north-facing half-circle at the mid level forms the generous, high cathedral-ceilinged hallway, with its exposed oregon beams, all-round glass windows, impressive stone pillared entrance, and heavy, old hardwood main door.

The much larger circle encompasses all three levels, with 10-foot-wide (3-meter) picture windows at the lower and mid-levels. Guest bedrooms, each with its own inspiring views and ensuite bathroom, are located on the lower level. The mid-level provides spacious, open-plan living, with a high, oregon-beamed cathedral ceiling. It includes the half-round Nook, a snuggly comfortable television viewing space. The impressive east-facing master bedroom and ensuite are also located mid-level.

The upper level is known as the Eyrie, or Eagle's Nest. It is smaller and serves the double function of office, with a semi-circular window desk, a meditation/quiet-time creative space, and built-in wall-to-windows lounge. The entire residence is finished in subtle, natural hues, directly reflecting the colors in the surrounding mountains and Lake Wakatipu. Despite its apparent remoteness, the house is located only ten minutes' drive from Queenstown.

Photography: Deb Gardner & Brooks

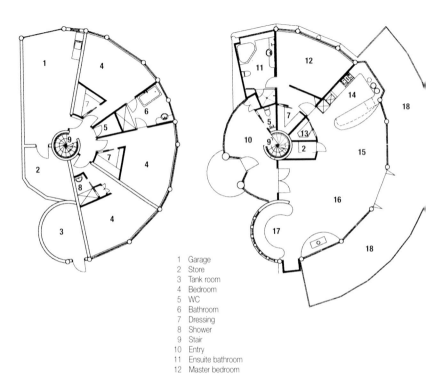

1 Garage
2 Store
3 Tank room
4 Bedroom
5 WC
6 Bathroom
7 Dressing
8 Shower
9 Stair
10 Entry
11 Ensuite bathroom
12 Master bedroom
13 Pantry
14 Kitchen
15 Dining
16 Living
17 Nook
18 Deck

Deamer Residence

San Francisco, California, USA
Mark English Architects

The location is a typical San Francisco doublewide lot, 50 feet x 100 feet deep (15 x 30 meters), sloping down from the street to the east. To the north is Buena Vista Park, a heavily wooded hill. To the east, an inspiring view sweeps from downtown San Francisco, across the Berkeley hills and Mount Diablo to the nearby rolling hills of Diamond Heights. The house consists of 4000 square feet (372 square meters), over four levels.

The clients are a mature San Francisco couple who love to cook and travel. Like many San Franciscans, they soon found their favorite "village" upon arrival in this city of villages. For them, the Mission district is a perfect melding of Italian Hilltown and funky seaside town.

The prospect of substantially changing an existing old home is, in San Francisco, fraught with controversy and conflict. The architects' approach to the process was to keep the neighbors aware of design progress through a schedule of meetings, starting with a wine and cheese affair on one of the original crumbling wood roof terraces. In the end this strategy worked and all public hearings were avoided. The design process was unusual: after an initial meeting, the basic building program was quickly established; soon after, three different explorations were prepared in computer model form. An animation was produced using the favorite solution, and approval followed shortly thereafter.

The interior materials include 18-inch (46-centimeter) square French limestone floors with radiant heating, cork floor tiles, anigre cabinets and built-ins, waxed and hammered copper backsplash, custom stainless sink, marble countertops and Brazilian cherry butcher-block island top. The exterior is finished with natural copper sheathing at the façade and roof deck solid rail, brass trellis, China jade slate terrace paving, and Brazilian cherry deck pallet system.

Desert Residence

Rancho Mirage, California, USA
Olson Sundberg Kundig Allen

This desert home is located on a ridge above an arroyo near Palm Springs. The owners wanted a house to serve as a gracious setting for living and entertaining. The surrounding desert landscape extends to the horizon with views taking in the Santa Rosa Mountains. Native desert plantings are cultivated to make a seamless transition from the site to the desert landscape. Solidity and mass, traditional desert construction concepts, are used to provide relief from the summer heat and harsh light. Windows are located under overhanging eaves or in deeply recessed openings to limit summer sun, but to allow the sun's lower winter light into the house's interior. The resulting building form, with its deep openings and voids, is sculpted in sunlight by strong light and dark shadows.

The house is designed as a series of offset colonnades, with the spaces between the walls providing the living area. The large-scale repetitive columns and beams run through the building and into the landscape, connecting the house to its environment. Inside, these columns also create architectural frames between which art is displayed. The material palette is kept simple and the colors neutral, reflecting the surrounding desert landscape. Roof planes are designed to float above the solid walls, allowing only reflected natural light to enter. Concrete is used for columns, interior wall forms and flooring. Smooth sand-colored plaster exterior walls and flat roofs connect the contemporary design to its desert precedents. Overhangs on the southern side shade floor-to-ceiling sliding doors to take advantage of the extremely pleasant winter climate.

Photography: Cindy Anderson, Benjamin Benschneider

Du Plessis House

Paraty, Rio de Janeiro, Brazil
Marcio Kogan Arquiteto

The house is located 9 miles (15 kilometers) from the historic city of Paraty, in Rio de Janeiro. The basic concept of the project was to explore architecture with a "double face": modern on the outside and conventional inside. Local regulations prescribed a tiled roof, which the architect integrated with his modernist approach.

The 4380-square-foot (407-square-meter) house is simply a large box faced with mineira stone (a stone from the Brazilian state of Minas Gerais), with a central external courtyard where four jaboticaba trees stand out from the swirled-pebbled paving. The exterior of the house, with its clay-tiled roof, looks modern, and fits in neatly with the requirements of the condominium estate in which it is located. Looking through the patio to the house reveals a more traditional interior design.

Four bedrooms and a small TV room are turned in to face the courtyard. All feature muxarabi wooden latticework from one end to another, which acts as a light filter. At night, seen from the courtyard when the lights of the rooms are on, this latticework covering is transformed into a glowing lantern.

The main room is turned out, facing the rear of the property, where the Atlantic rainforest begins. All the doors can be opened and the room joins a bamboo-covered terrace and the swimming pool beyond. An opening in the courtyard frames views of the estate's golf course.

East St Kilda Residence

East St Kilda, Victoria, Australia
Inarc Architects

This expansive home was designed for a large and growing family devoted to the aesthetics of contemporary design. This duality of purpose between the modernist aesthetic and everyday family use is visible in the façades: the public face is a formal gray stone composition while the private face is a warmer timber-clad skin.

The totally transparent ground and first-floor windows are well disguised and hidden from the street, and give no indication as to the internal function, providing both anonymity and uniformity when the building is performing its extended family duties. These large areas of glass allow an intimate relationship with the landscape and garden vistas. Significant integration between the architecture and engineering was required to achieve the fenestration patterns on the first floor. Design features such as the highly rationalized external elevations, flat roof profiles, and minimal ground floor walls required the integration of innovative structural solutions.

The ground floor provides a public forum as well as a family living domain. Because of the flatness of the site and the lack of distant views, internal axes are introduced to control the sight lines within the property and to give focus at the end of long hallways.

The study has direct access to the entry for the reception of visitors, as well as a northern outlook onto a private courtyard garden. Beyond the study is the guest suite with its own bathroom and dressing area. Similar to the study, it is discreetly removed from the family living and bedroom areas, and has its own private outlook to the rear garden.

A large sitting area and an adjacent dining area can be divided or opened up by panels that slide back into nib walls. Large sliding glass doors allow these spaces to spill out onto the courtyards and gardens.

The kitchen opens onto its own courtyard at the front of the house, which in turn acts as an informal outdoor eating area as well as a play area for younger children with direct supervision from the kitchen.

The first floor accommodates all the bedrooms and bathrooms for the family. The children's bedrooms are arranged along the front elevation of the house, and are linked by an axial gallery that mirrors the main circulation axis on the ground floor. The main bedroom is a separate suite with an adjoining nursery.

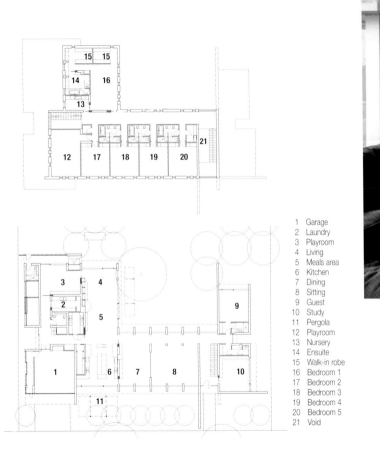

1 Garage
2 Laundry
3 Playroom
4 Living
5 Meals area
6 Kitchen
7 Dining
8 Sitting
9 Guest
10 Study
11 Pergola
12 Playroom
13 Nursery
14 Ensuite
15 Walk-in robe
16 Bedroom 1
17 Bedroom 2
18 Bedroom 3
19 Bedroom 4
20 Bedroom 5
21 Void

Ecevit House

Potomac, Maryland, USA
McInturff Architects

Sited on a wooded slope adjacent to a meadow in
Maryland's horse country, this house connects to
the local farm vernacular through its simplicity of
siting, form and detail. A straightforward L-shaped
plan creates an entry court between the
garage/service wing and the house proper, where
a great room on the first floor is oriented to take
advantage of views into a wooded ravine to the
north. South light is brought into the house
through selective fenestration toward the
approach road and clerestory windows beneath
shed roofs whose bracketed eaves support
generous overhangs while referring to nearby
barns. Finally, a screened porch pavilion flies off
the body of the house projecting the eye, and the
occupants, into the woods beyond.

Photography: Julia Heine

Edgewater

Short Hills, New Jersey, USA
WESKetch Architecture

Locating a new home in a historic suburb that abuts a lake is quite a challenge architecturally, especially when the home is meant to look as though it has always been there. The clients were living in a developer home and desired a home that portrayed their inner style while maintaining historic detail and charm.

The views to the east and north were important and creating privacy on a corner lot was imperative. An L-shaped parti resulted from the restraints of the corner lot. By addressing both streets and keeping true to the constricting setbacks, the home has windows and ventilation on two or three sides of all rooms. The effect is a home with many detailed rooms and a plan that allows the home to sprawl around the corner. This home has a sense of permanence and character that exudes warmth through its finely hand-crafted brick façade and intricately detailed eaves and window placement.

The heart and soul of the home can be found on the interior where the English Arts and Crafts era-inspired details allow the spaces to stand alone and still flow gracefully from one room to the next. The European Craftsman elements of this home are rich with detail and many famous architects such as Edwin Lutyens helped to create this building by inspiring scale, detail and use of materials. Such details include the stacked brick

quoining at the front entry aligning so carefully with all horizontal lines of the façade, custom-made European-style mahogany windows, and exposed rough-sawn cedar rafter tails with hand crafted half-round copper gutters at the eaves.

Every detail was checked and rechecked to accurately portray the historic details of the past, including the hand-made clay roof tiles from France. Despite being heavily influenced by English Craftsman designs of the past, the house is overlaid with the most-up-to date, high-performance building techniques.

Photography: Jay Rosenblatt Photography

Ehrlich Residence

Santa Monica, California, USA
John Friedman Alice Kimm Architects, Inc.

The main challenge of this house was to resolve a contradiction between the clients' wishes and the site itself. The clients wanted a sustainable house, optimally a south-facing structure with a thin profile to encourage maximum cross-breezes and sunlight penetration. At the same time, they wanted the living spaces to open onto the largest possible walled garden which, due to the city codes, was on the northeast side of the property.

The resulting first-floor plan shows an L-shaped series of living spaces wrapped around the garage and opening onto an L-shaped garden. On the southeast side, overhanging eaves block the summer sun, but allow the winter sun to heat up the concrete floor, which acts as a heat sink. The southwest façade is mostly solid to keep out the punishing western sun; the koi pond surrounding the living room cools the breezes that enter the main living spaces. The house is clad primarily with smooth-troweled plaster and shiplapped cement board, both in a subtle range of natural tones.

Strategies were developed to obtain the effects of a thin, south-facing house even though the main living areas face northeast. Hidden in the relatively strict orthogonal layout is a series of diagonals in plan and section that bring in wind and light from the south. A dramatic example is the monitor-like opening which can be seen on the second floor and whose eave faces due south. Created by dispersing the solid, service elements of the house to create a "diagonal void," during the winter it brings direct light to the furthest northern corner of the house. Just as importantly, this internal massing (as opposed to the more common external massing) creates an atrium space that not only contains the stair, but also vents the hot air of the house through a pair of motorized skylights in the roof.

The atrium has several roles beyond its sustainable function: its verticality contrasts with the compressed horizontality of much of the first floor, intensifying the interior's relationship with the garden. Its mixture of reflected and direct light tracks the sun during the day, and emits a lantern-like glow at night. The atrium also organizes the rooms on the second floor, particularly the master bedroom, which has an internal window that allows the clients to take in the ever-changing light in the double-height space. Situated to block noise from the busy boulevard, the master bathroom takes advantage of this quality with light from three different orientations.

Photography: Benny Chan, Fotoworks

Ford Residence

Denver, Colorado, USA
Hutton Ford Architects

The homeowners, both architects, decided to expand their home, built in 1896, to accommodate a growing family. The program included renovating and expanding the kitchen, adding a family room and breakfast area and a second-floor master bedroom, to create a 2700-square-foot (250-square-meter) home.

The architecture of the addition is derivative of the original home while providing a modern sensibility; the goal was a seamless integration between old and new. Underlying organizing principles found in the 1896 architecture are incorporated into the addition: datums expressed as projected brick bands that organize windows and brick arches, masonry details, roof slopes and vertical proportions.

The contemporary interior utilizes structural elements and varied ceiling planes to define space and direct the eye. Low-cost materials such as gypsum board add to the simple expression. This honest expression is evident at the second-floor bedroom where the roof and structural forms define the character of the space. Six dormers overhead in the interior of the bedroom help to define various zones, including a natural canopy over the bed. The dormers also serve to provide a dynamic quality to the space with ceiling heights varying from 3 to 15 feet (1 to 4.5 meters). Paired structural columns help to subdivide the bedroom into distinct zones for sleeping and washing. The exterior wall is pushed and pulled to create areas for window seats at the first and second floor.

At the main level, the floor of the new family room is 16 inches (41 centimeters) lower than the existing main floor to provide an 11-foot (3.4-meter) ceiling. Soffits and arches are used to provide rhythm, define space and take the eye to the sandstone fireplace at the south wall. The roof and ceiling also step up at the fireplace to give a sense of visual lift and direct the eye upwards along the tapered lines of the fireplace, terminating in ridge skylights, which wash the sandstone in natural light. Full height windows frame the fireplace. Also at the south wall, the exterior Flemish bond brick with its recessed header pattern is continued inside and out to provide color and texture. The structural columns between the family room and the kitchen areas create an arched entry feature and provide rhythm and a visual break at the point where the floor level changes.

Photography: Ron Johnson; Jackie Shumaker

Fritz Residence

Palm Desert, California, USA
OJMR Architects

The house is located on a flat, irregularly shaped lot at the end of a cul-de-sac. The neighborhood contains a variety of styles and references to the preferred typical suburban desert subdivision architecture.

The 2600-square-foot (242-square-meter) house was designed for a retired couple with the need for guest bedroom suites and a large communal space for the living, dining, and kitchen areas.

To achieve a feeling of "simplicity" within conventional means, it was decided that planning and construction must be straightforward, and the character of the house reflect a strategy of enclosure and openness focused toward the main outdoor space. Two simple volumes are connected together to define a corner, with one wing containing the guest bedrooms, and the other containing the master suite. The two wings are connected at the main living, dining, and kitchen space.

Hallways are located along the east and south sides of the two wings and help to define the laterally situated rooms, which can be closed off from the circulation zone with large sliding walls. The rooms all access the outdoor pool/courtyard space from large sliding glass walls.

Materials incorporated in this project include exposed concrete block walls, natural stone veneer walls, plaster over wood framing, concrete floors, walnut cabinetry, Gascogne blue limestone floors in bathrooms, translucent glass panels, Montauk black marble counters in the kitchen, and Venetino white marble countertops in the bathroom and on the kitchen island.

Photography: Ciro Coelho

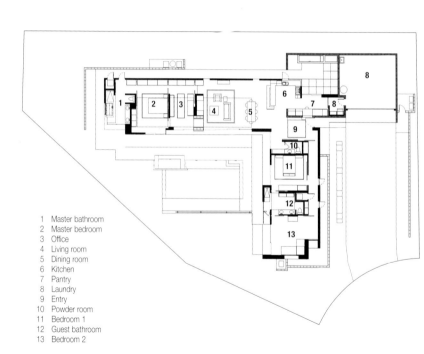

1   Master bathroom
2   Master bedroom
3   Office
4   Living room
5   Dining room
6   Kitchen
7   Pantry
8   Laundry
9   Entry
10 Powder room
11 Bedroom 1
12 Guest bathroom
13 Bedroom 2

Gama Issa House

Alto de Pinheiros, São Paulo, Brazil
Marcio Kogan Architect

The architect's diary note: São Paulo, 21 January, 2002:

"It is ten o'clock at night. Very hot. I use this moment of rare calm and solitude to design the new house. I look through the window and parked in front of the building is a BMW X5. A young man of about 27 slides out of the car with a stunning blonde fearfully clutching her Prada bag. An almost-black, almost-beggar approaches asking if he can watch the car for R$5. They go into a Japanese restaurant. On the radio, which I will turn off within ten seconds, there is talk of the most recent kidnapping and a prison rebellion. I read my notes of the first meeting with the clients, a couple in advertising. We spoke of an enormous library in the living room with double-height ceilings, enormous windows opening completely to the garden, a 10 x 100-foot (3 x 30-meter) pool, a kitchen with an orange lunch table in the center, two symmetrical marble staircases lit by focused natural light, a precisely detailed work studio, spaces of rare and elegant proportions which always relate to the exterior differently, white textures, a Eero Aarnio ball club chair, minimalism, the 60s, electronic music, Stockhausen, Cage, the latest issue of Visionaire magazine, a recipe for spaghetti al mare and finally, 'My Uncle' by Jacques Tati.

I think of a single enormous volume wrapping everything: a white box. In São Paulo, we don't need to be concerned about environmental coherence, it is total chaos, the most absolute chaos. In this city, the world's ugliest, which overflows energy, vibrant like no other, loved and hated, anything that is projected will be totally integrated into the city. Ah, yes, don't let me forget an enormous wall protecting the house, covered in natural wood (maybe from the last tree of the Amazon), and which, certainly, will be completely covered by graffiti, giving the final touch in perfect harmony with the environment."

Glazer Residence

Colorado, USA
Appleton & Associates, Inc. – Architects

The challenge was to create a fun, entertaining vacation retreat for our client's family and friends. The project included an extensive program for a main house, two separate guesthouses, a caretaker's unit and horse barn.

The family compound takes advantage of the magnificent panoramic views, and also has a vernacular presence on the site, reminiscent of an old ranch homestead or mining camp, as if it had grown and been added to over the years. To reduce the impact of the scale of the project and fit it harmoniously on the site, the mass of the large main house was broken into several separate but interconnected gabled, barn-like buildings, with a main entry stair tower that looked like it might have once been a grain silo. Principal material choices were in keeping with the old ranch idea, utilizing standing seam metal roofing, and salvaged barn timbers and siding. The stone base

and site walls were designed to appear like ruins, suggesting that the place may have been reconstructed on an older masonry foundation. Salvaged barn wood was also recycled for the interior doors, millwork, trim and cabinetry.

In the interior, the octagonal stair tower was conceived as a fantasy tree house, with the splitlog stair winding its way up around eight interior tree columns made from standing dead Lodgepole pines. The bark was left intact, and dead branches were added to hold hanging lanterns, bird nests, carved animals and other surprises, as well as serving as the stair railing. The finished compound is full of rough-hewn, Wild West romance and nostalgia, but its construction and reliance on salvaged and recycled materials are also environmentally conscientious decisions to which we were committed from the start.

Photography: Alex Vertikoff

Hope Ranch Residence

Santa Barbara, California, USA
Shubin + Donaldson Architects, Adler Arquitectos

Hope Ranch is a former working ranch that has been subdivided into equestrian oriented, mostly Western ranch-style estates.

This project included the new construction of a 7500-square-foot (697-square-meter) primary residence and a 3000-square-foot (280-square-meter) pool structure for the client and his family. A "contemporary house with a Mexican flavor" is what the art-collecting client requested. The architects responded with a contextual mélange of multiple orthogonal volumes that reflect a refined Mexican spirit in shape and material. The solidity of forms on one side of the home speaks to the Mexican flavor of the structure, while the abundance of glazing on the other side relates to the physical context of the coastal site.

The rough plaster of the 18-inch-thick (45-centimeter) walls—the same finish seen often in Mexico—adds texture and depth, and softens the monumentality of the forms. Although in the vein of Mexican architecture, this home departs in the choice of color, with a decidedly neutral, earthy pigment. Contrasting with the rough forms is the limestone-clad entry volume that appears to slice through the plaster volumes. The entry separates the home's public and private spaces.

Responding to the site, the architects created a constant interplay between indoor and outdoor in a continual effort to frame views and compose angles. Upon entering the building, beyond the play of forms, is the surprise view through the entry toward the negative-edge reflecting pool and out to the ocean beyond. Large, floor-to-ceiling windows wrap around a fountain, which also brings light into the home. One can go from the living room to the dining room across the stepping stones in the central reflecting pool.

An indoor swimming pool is accessed down the stairs from the master suite through a curved corridor that sports a rare hint of vibrant color. A deep orange curving corridor and sparkling blue wall in the pool house are a nod to the traditional Mexican palette. Three skylights punctuate the space that houses a 60-foot-long (18-meter) lap pool.

The owners wanted the house to have public spaces for social events. The dramatic open foyer and entry create a seamless experience for visitors as they journey from exterior to interior. Exterior limestone is repeated in the flooring, with contrasting darker limestone stripes echoing the ceiling articulation. Mexican tzalam wood is used for the custom-made doors, the spectacular interior bridge, and the interior wood floors.

Photography: Ciro Coelho

House for GOA

Sunshine Coast, Queensland, Australia
Bligh Voller Nield Pty Ltd

The brief for this holiday home on Australia's Sunshine Coast called for a contemporary interpretation of traditional tropical Pacific architecture. The clients were keen to explore and exploit the characteristics offered by the contemporary and traditional tropical architecture of Southeast Asia and sub-tropical Australia in a local setting.

The design responds to the existing house's footprint and fan-shaped site in a manner that maximizes site usage. The narrow street frontage opens out to the rear of the site, allowing the design to focus on the view over the water beyond. Entering the house through the street-side gatehouse and confined entry corridor, the drama of the open living spaces and canal view is concealed from the street. The U-shaped plan enhances the sense of privacy from the street and neighbors, allowing the creation of a central courtyard space that links the living spaces at ground level. This roofed courtyard with associated swimming pool and pond creates a focal point for the house over both levels, drawing the eye out to the water beyond.

The upper-floor bedrooms are oriented around a generous central stair void with an associated skylight through which natural light filters into the deeper parts of the house. From the upper-floor bedrooms, large opening glass doors direct the view out over the crafted shingled roof of the arcaded court below.

The orientation of the site toward the canal demanded a strong response to the impact of the western sun. The use of deep outdoor rooms (lanai and bale) to the west combined with operable sunshading blinds, shutters, and screens has ensured both shading and privacy.

The use of timber, stone, glass, copper, bamboo, and natural textiles has resulted in a highly tactile and relaxed house, ideal for coastal living.

The 6240-square-foot (580-square-meter) building maximizes site usage without compromising on the desired "tropical" quality within the house. This requirement of the client to feel "exposed to the elements" has been enhanced by a careful integration of dense landscaping, water features, diffused skylights, and natural materials.

Photography: David Sandison

House for the Future

Museum of Welsh Life, St Fagans, Cardiff, Wales, UK

Jestico + Whiles
(Heinz Richardson, Jude Harris, Andy Piles)

The National Museums and Galleries of Wales and BBC Wales commissioned a new house to stand alongside a collection of historic buildings, which comprise the Museum of Welsh Life at St Fagans, near Cardiff in Wales. The structure consists of a post-and-beam timber frame prefabricated with locally grown oak. A super-insulated wall of timber studwork wraps around three sides of the building, allowing maximum flexibility for window and door openings. This is faced externally with lime render and Welsh oak boarding. Sheep's wool in the walls and recycled newspapers in the roof provide high levels of insulation.

The house relies on a strategy of sensible energy use, assisted by passive technologies that are supported by easy-to-use control systems. It has been designed to make no net contribution to carbon dioxide emissions. It is highly insulated and

features a ground source heat pump and a wood pellet heater, as well as passive solar gain supply heating. An active solar (water heating) and photovoltaic unit mounted at ridge level contribute to the power and hot water demands.

Planning of the internal living space is kept deliberately fluid to respond to the particular needs of the residents. Open living and daytime spaces are located to the south, while more private and enclosed cellular spaces are located to the north. The modular approach to the design allows the possibility for a number of variations to the base model according to spatial needs, a desire for flexibility, and available finance. A simple shell structure can be increasingly colonized as the circumstances of the residents alter with time and economics.

Photography: courtesy National Museums and Galleries of Wales

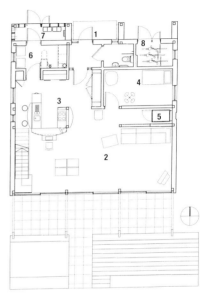

1 Entrance
2 Living/dining
3 Kitchen area
4 Study bedroom
5 Lift
6 Utility
7 Recycling
8 Store

165

House of Silence

Finland
Juhani Pallasmaa Architects

This vacation house and sauna, on an exceptionally beautiful lakeside site, was designed as a retreat for the family and guests of a musician and a director of an art center in Eastern Finland.

The house proper contains an ample living room, double-height library, kitchen–dining area, bathroom and service facilities on the ground level, and three bedrooms upstairs along a suspended corridor which terminates in a screened and skylit porch above the terrace of the main floor.

The sauna structure contains a skylit dressing room with a fireplace and kitchenette, sauna and shower room. The partly covered outdoor area toward the house is used to store firewood, and the terrace in the opposite end contains a wood-lined Japanese bath tub sunk into the floor. The ensemble is completed by a wooden pier, a service building painted black in the middle of a group of boulders, and a future teahouse on top of the rocky hill behind the house proper.

The buildings with their multitude of openings are conceived to orchestrate views and light, like a cinematic montage: as the concrete wall of the sauna pushes into the ground, the skylight through the turf roof allows a view of the tree tops; the glass roof above the staircase allows views of the forest behind.

The structure is a combination of steel tube columns and wood structures. The exterior of the house is treated with tar, matched with the orange color of pine bark; the sauna is tarred black to deepen the impression of earth and shadow. The interior surfaces of the house are stained bone white; the sauna interiors are entirely of untreated red alder. All building components, with the exception of hinges and door pulls, were custom-made by local carpenters.

The project was given its name, House of Silence, in the course of the construction as it became evident that the interplay of nature and architecture enabled the dweller to recover the precious silence of his/her soul.

Photography: Rauno Träskelin

1 Entrance hall
2 Living room
3 Dining room
4 Kitchen
5 Library
6 Terrace
7 Courtyard
8 Sauna terrace
9 Dressing/restroom
10 Shower room
11 Sauna
12 Master bedroom
13 Bedroom
14 Outdoor terrace
15 Void above living room
16 Void above library
17 Glass roof above entrance

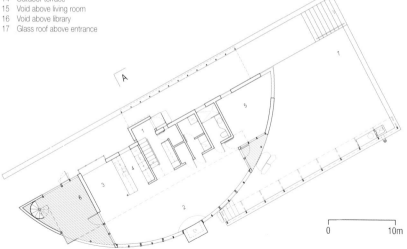

0   10m

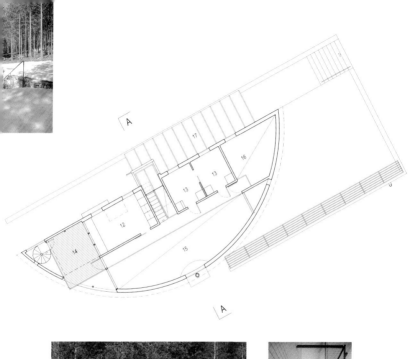

169

171

Iporanga House

Iporanga Beach, São Paulo, Brazil
Sandra Picciotto Architecture and Interiors

Young and demanding clients wanted a stylish and comfortable house, but their main wish was for a beach house that looked as if it belonged in the jungle.

The challenge for the architect was to create a new house, but to retain the prefabricated steel structure already on the site. A further difficulty was encountered in relation to the carpentry and the supply of wood for the house. The wood was eventually sourced from Para in the north of Brazil, and modified to provide the effects desired by the architect. The wood provides the element of rusticity desired by the clients, and it will continue to weather and change in appearance.

Doors and window frames were carefully designed to capture the expansive views; water and plants were thoughtfully incorporated into the design of the house.

Despite its large size (5380 square feet/500 square meters), the house is harmonious, simple and sophisticated, in keeping with its beachside location.

Photography: Tuca Reinés

Kew House

Kew, Victoria, Australia
Jackson Clements Burrows Architects

The Kew House is located on an existing subdivided tennis court cut into a steep site in Melbourne's inner east. The brief called for car access, and for the master bedroom and living areas to be located on the same level.

The brief provided an opportunity to design a building that immersed itself into its context, not as a stand-alone inanimate object, but as a building that contributed to and formed part of the surrounding ambiance. If the ground plane (existing tennis court) was an artificial scar on the landscape, could the new building effect a new condition that repaired, rejuvenated and reconnected with what once was? Could a built solution contribute to the ambiance of an existing location by intensifying its intangible ephemeral qualities? How do you make a building that shifts the focal point from architecture to the atmosphere it produces? These questions informed the built solution, the selection of materials, the articulation of interior volumes and the resolution of the architectural form itself.

The first-floor living platform, suspended amongst a canopy of trees and supported by a steel column system, recalls the new growth of self-seeded saplings. The two-tone cladding of the architectural form evokes the colors of the once-dominant indigenous river red gums and the satin finish of the Colorbond contrasts with the dull matt of oxidizing zinc. These are materials that accentuate the liveliness of the constant changes in the light.

The house responds to all orientations in a specific way. Every room in the house orients itself north to maximize a view corridor across the nearby golf course and the northern suburbs of Melbourne. The west and east openings are kept to a minimum, reducing heat gain and overlooking to neighboring properties and protecting the occupants from the impact of future development on both east and west boundaries.

The use of a detailed steel structure and metal building products in this project as structural and cladding elements was central to achieving the architectural intention of the project—a response that references, heals, regenerates, and strengthens both the physical and atmospheric qualities of its site and surrounds.

Photography: John Gollings, courtesy Jackson Clements Burrows

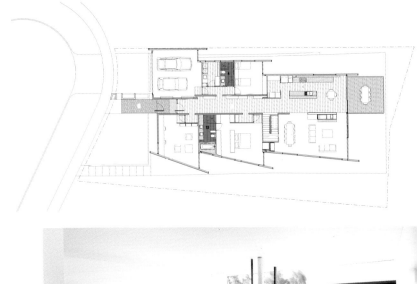

Kimber House

Perth, Western Australia, Australia
Patroni Architects

The foremost item of the brief was the tennis court and this became the context for the project as the game of tennis and its device became an analogy for the program—a modern family with demands for fluctuating numbers and a variety of lifestyles. The spaces both within and outside the house flow like an exploded tennis court; the tramline-like spine wall allows a variety of family configurations to optimally enjoy the place at one time.

All north-facing glass is shaded by cantilevered shade structures that permit winter sun and exclude summer sun. There are very few openings to the east or west. The boundary between inside and outside has been deliberately blurred. The shifting levels allow one space to "float" while another space seems to be firmly earthed; the living areas extend beyond the pivoting timber doors without changing level or material, and then begin to terrace down past the swimming pool, via a lily pond that reveals itself as the roof of the tennis court pavilion. The water garden is let in using long, low windows at floor level, excluding the view of an adjoining property while allowing the reflected light of the moving water to animate the interior of the apartment side of the house, emphasizing its "floating" quality. By day, the house is flooded with natural light; at night lighting is used both inside and out to emphasize the integration between the two.

The architectural language of the project is different from its neighbors, some of which were designed 80–90 years ago, while some contemporary houses are imitations of, or references to past styles. It was our intention that the project be proudly of its time, helping to log architectural development from the past, present and future. The local authority did not share this position and the project did not receive planning consent for 12 months, and then only via ministerial appeal. Nevertheless, the project is in scale with its neighbors and an overall integration with the neighborhood and its character has been achieved, while also making a vibrant contribution to the streetscape.

Photography: Robert Frith

185

Leesa and Sam's House

Christmas Lake, Excelsior, Minnesota, USA

Charles R. Stinson Architects

Leesa Nahki-Brown, a mother with a preteen son, had a simple wish: "I wanted a home that we could really live in and where Sam would feel good bringing his friends." She also specified a small office space, a laundry next to the bedrooms, a built-in buffet, kitchen island, and unique fireplace. The two-bedroom lakeside house is a De Stijl-like composition of sophisticated simplicity, Modrianesque planes of primary colors juxtaposed with white, and open space filled with light. Two-story windows in a square arch allow views straight through the white-stucco house to the lake, with overhangs positioned to allow in light during the winter and block hot sun in the summer.

"Leesa asked us to design the interiors and she wanted color," Stinson says, "so we did an abstraction of primary colors and made a Modrian composition out of them". One early winter morning during construction, he saw the main level aglow with light from the rising sun reflected off the lake. "When sun came into the great room, the space was transformed into a golden temple," he recalls, "so we built on this experience using bamboo floors and painting the ceiling a deep yellow to extend that golden moment." Color is also found on the main level in the red-painted forms of the glass-block-framed fireplace. On the other end of the first floor are the dining room and kitchen, separated by a built-in floating buffet with a glass plane intersected by vertical square arch shelving that echoes the fireplace composition across the room.

The square arch theme is also found in the white Corian that wraps the maple cabinets and the built-in flower vase holder atop the curved-maple butcher block and black-granite island. A small study is located behind the kitchen. The entire first floor opens onto a patio overlooking the lawn extending to the lake. The second level includes two bedrooms separated by a daylit gallery. Sam's small suite contains a walk-in closet and bath. Leesa's suite includes a fireplace framed with green-painted forms and white walls. Off their bedrooms, mother and son share a large balcony that overlooks the lake.

Photography: Peter Bastianelli Kerze

Montecito Residence

Montecito, California, USA
Shubin + Donaldson Architects

Situated in Montecito, California, an upscale hillside community adjacent to Santa Barbara, this residence is one of few contemporary designs in the area. The clients, a retired couple, desired a restrained and economical building in which to enjoy their substantial art collection, and the dynamic site that features mountain and ocean views. The architects' goal was to design a contemporary, urban, loft-like home in a very traditional neighborhood. The three-bedroom residence is distinctly organized with one main axis or circulation/gallery that runs along the whole structure. The center of the building features the public areas of living, dining, and kitchen, with circulation walls functioning as the desired gallery space for artwork. The open plan emphasizes space usage and contemporary living. A sculptural glass-and-steel fireplace separates the living area from the dining room. The far north-end block serves as the master bedroom and bath. The two-bedroom guest quarters are at the opposite end, adjacent to a three-car garage.

A modern and inviting environment was achieved by layering the mix of building and finish materials, by maintaining a constant visual connection with the outdoors, and by flooding the spaces with light, with the aid of ten skylights throughout. The dwelling is covered by a shed roof built with steel trusses and metal decking. This structure is revealed at the dramatic entry and along the main axis circulation/gallery to express its place within the overall design vocabulary. The walls of the house are primarily plaster and glass. Maple flooring and cabinetry add warmth and intimacy to the public areas, while subtle hues of tinted plaster soften the composition of intersecting planes on the interior and exterior.

Photography: Tom Bonner

Mountain Cabin

California, USA
Walker Warner Architects

The clients' love for this beautiful mountainous region began many years before they decided to build a weekend cabin there. Their wish was that the buildings would be as minimal in size as possible, respecting the land and the pace of life that unfolds there. They asked that the indoor/outdoor connections be maximized so that rooms could borrow space and beauty from the surrounding landscape. They envisioned a cabin that would slip into the landscape as if it had always been there, and always would be. This cabin would be passed down through the family from generation to generation.

The architects' goal was to make the cabin as flexible and efficient as possible. Rooms were designed to spill out into the site with 10-foot-wide (3-meter) sets of doors opening to the meadow. Communal living spaces in the cabin were created to provide more expansive spaces for nighttime activities. The bulk of the cabin was reduced by employing built-ins throughout, to give rooms ship-like efficiency, and by lowering plate heights to make rooms cozy and intimate. Doors and windows push dormers above the main roof plane where necessary and fill between members of the timber frame to give the cabin a strong sense of connection between indoors and out. As a result, no room feels crowded. Each shares the expansiveness of the immediate and distant views beyond.

The material palette and detailing were approached with three goals: to allow the site and cabin to flow into one another, to use environmentally sourced materials, and to give the cabin a sense of permanence. The material palette was reduced to essentials: wood, steel, and stone. The materials appear both on the interior and the exterior of the cabin, blurring the line between inside and out. Minimal detailing allows the full beauty of the materials to be revealed without the distraction of fussy details. A timber frame was an ideal solution to a short building season and the desire to use reclaimed material. Additionally, stone was salvaged from a ranch where a quarry had been abandoned a hundred years ago. Granite that had been split and then left to weather in the elements was carefully installed to expose its natural patina. Artisans were brought in to share their special talents. Custom elements, from light fixtures to sinks carved from blocks of stone, give the cabin the feeling of a rare gem.

Photography: César Rubio

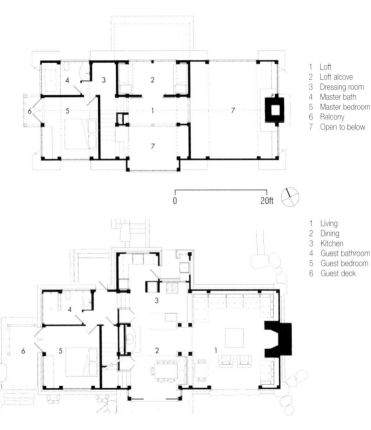

1 Loft
2 Loft alcove
3 Dressing room
4 Master bath
5 Master bedroom
6 Balcony
7 Open to below

0   20ft

1 Living
2 Dining
3 Kitchen
4 Guest bathroom
5 Guest bedroom
6 Guest deck

Nautilus

Rancho Mirage, California, USA
Patel Architecture; Narendra Patel, AIA

Approaching the house, the captivating sculptural form, natural materials, soft desert colors and curving walls gently guide the visitor through the metal gates into the front courtyard. Natural stone-faced walls are set off against simple elegant stucco forms, emphasizing form and volume.

The drama is intensified as one walks through the front door. Walls begin sweeping from the outside, through the transparent glass barriers inside and back again, and out the other end to the water view. The hovering vaulted ceiling creates the illusion of a floating cover to this indoor/outdoor visual living experience. The inspiration for this house came to the architect from a seashell. The mathematical formula from the DaVinci code and the conical shape of the nautilus became the inspiration and derivation for his translation of this home's design.

The 5900-square-foot (550-square-meter) home comprises a master bedroom with his-and-her bathrooms and closets, a living room with sunken bar, dining room, kitchen leading to family room, an office, a second bedroom, a large gym, and a complete guest house. A 1000-square-foot (93-square-meter), three-car garage completes the program.

All interior walls are covered with Venetian plaster. The natural stone wall continues from the outside, penetrating the glass wall barrier as it flows through the living room. The roof is copper and the floors limestone. The ceiling is tongue-and-groove wood, punctured with myriad small halogen lights producing the effect of a star-studded sky.

The floating ceiling effect is achieved by steel columns and beams combined with open web steel bar trusses and wood framing. This is accentuated by exterior walls, which are separated from this large vault by clerestory windows and the intermediary dividing walls, freestanding and much lower than the curved ceiling itself. An illusion of space and volume, with the outdoor sky visible from all directions, creates the effect of a seemingly free-standing roof.

This home was designed using the principles of sustainable design, resulting in a building that is environmentally responsible and a healthy place to live. This was achieved by implementing energy efficient lighting, heat and cooling; specifying environmentally friendly green building and construction methods; orienting the glazed area and living spaces to achieve low energy usage; installation of plumbing fixtures with reduced water usage; and the introduction of native arid landscaping, to achieve water savings.

Photography: Arthur Coleman

No. 4

Andalucia, Spain
Thomas de Cruz Architects/Designers;
Roach & Partners Developers

Designed by London-based architect Peter Thomas de Cruz, this spectacular contemporary house occupies a hillside site inland from the coast of southern Spain. The brainchild of the developers, the house challenges the orthodoxy of much of the recent pseudo-vernacular development in the area with calm, flowing spaces, a considered response to topography and climate and simplicity in detail.

With stunning views across a valley toward distant mountains in the west, this largely single-aspect house uses the slope of the site to maximum advantage. The core of the house is a top-lit, double-height gallery flooded with natural light that runs across the slope of the site. The prime living spaces are on the west side of the gallery while to the east, ancillary accommodation and cooling courtyards are set into the hillside. All of the full-height glazed façades parallel with the slope open fully to allow air to pass through the building, making the most of anabatic and katabatic winds. The cross ventilation, combined with large cantilevered roof overhangs and balconies which provide solar shading, reduces the reliance on air conditioning and extends the opportunity for comfortable open air living.

From the entrance, an elliptical curved wall on the west side peels away from the main axis, widening the gallery and pulling you toward a double-height window at the end, progressively revealing a single mountain peak in the distance. Punched holes in the gallery wall give glimpses of mountain views to the west across the series of interconnected open plan living spaces. The end of the gallery culminates in a large double-height living space that leads toward a disappearing edge swimming pool, which projects out into space. At first-floor level, a bridge open on both sides overlooking the main living space leads to the master bedroom suite, which is connected to a private study below by a spiral staircase wrapped within the "tail" of the curved wall.

Adding to the sense of spectacle, the house is dramatically cut in two, with a glass-floored dining space bridging the gap between the two halves and linking the cooking space to the living space. The parallel gallery sits astride an internal pool and, when all the glazing is fully retracted, both the gallery and the dining space become bridges fully open to the air. The calmness of the house is accentuated by water flowing from the gallery courtyard pool down over a slate-finished waterfall beneath the dining room to meet the lowest of the two connected swimming pools.

Photography: Simon Cuss

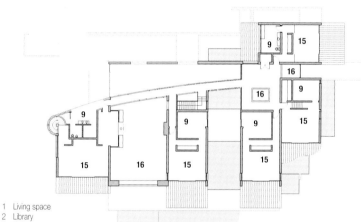

1   Living space
2   Library
3   Dining space
4   Kitchen
5   Gallery
6   Downstairs bedroom
7   Utility room
8   Internet room
9   Bathroom
10 Pantry
11 Study
12 Guest bedroom
13 Swimming pool
14 Pool
15 Bedroom
16 Void

Orleans House

Cape Cod, Massachusetts, USA
Charles Rose Architects Inc

The 6-acre (2.5-hectare) site is located on a bluff overlooking Pleasant Bay, Nauset Beach, and the Atlantic Ocean. The house, which traces and reinforces a naturally occurring bowl in the landscape, is sited on a slight ridge, gaining water views and protecting the inland landscape. The L-shaped organization of the house creates an intimate entry landscape and orients a series of rooms to the water and southern light.

The southern wing of the 6000-square-foot (557-square-meter) house is a spacious single-level volume: the foyer, gallery, living room, dining room, and kitchen open onto each other but remain distinct with stepped floor levels and deliberately positioned walls for art. The south and west edges of the main house spill into the landscape as a series of stepped exterior terraces. Roof overhangs and sunscreen trellises shelter and shade interior and exterior spaces. At the knuckle of the L is the vertical spine of the house, an open stair providing light and access to the wine cellar, the guest bedroom levels, and an upper sitting room nested beneath a roof monitor.

To the west of the main house is a tower structure with a second floor office: this room captures sweeping views to the north, east, and south. The family room is linked to the house by a covered walk, which also serves to shield the parking area from the entry landscape. A guesthouse is sited on a knoll to the north. A painting studio on the ground floor has large rolling barn doors opening to the south and the view.

Photography: John Edward Linden

Oshry Residence

Bel Air, California, USA

Zoltan E. Pali, FAIA; Studio Pali Fekete Architects (SPF:a)

The site for the Oshry Residence was the inspiration for the project's design, requiring creative solutions to complex environmental factors. Strict zoning guidelines for hillside lots, poor soil conditions, dynamic programmatic requirements, desired adjacencies, and wide panoramic views posed critical challenges to the building's occupation of the site, but both client and architect envisioned the remarkable possibilities that the site offered, if the challenges could be overcome. The combined interaction of these forces resulted in a linear building configuration of two enfilade blocks connected by a bridge across a minimally landscaped courtyard. Given the size of the program (5000 square feet/465 square meters), the program offered an opportunity to integrate the outdoors into the building through a series of interior/exterior spatial penetrations. In addition, the longitudinal orientation of the house vis-à-vis the site created a highly charged east elevation, and numerous vantage points from within the house across the dramatic landscape below.

The Oshry Residence façade is straightforwardly articulated, boldly featuring the clean volumetric and programmatic elements of the structure. It is from the internal strip of space, parallel to the east façade, that one orients oneself physically within the house and visually to the surroundings. Elements such as the circulation bridge, stone

screen wall, and retracting wood panels are derived from this organization. The end result is a scheme that resolves the inherent complexities of the site with the desired living conditions of the client, and furthers existing notions of materiality and transparency with seamless integration.

The house integrates major design elements with passive shading and ventilation functions, for maximum energy efficiency. Stone louvers on the first floor shade the living room without obstructing views. The glass bridge on the second floor uses operable windows that can be opened during hotter days, letting the warmer air escape from the second-story space, quickly cooling the rooms below.

Photography: John Linden

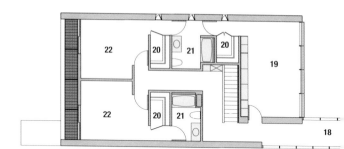

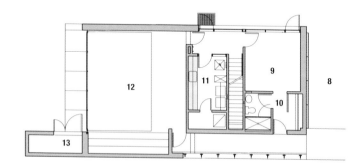

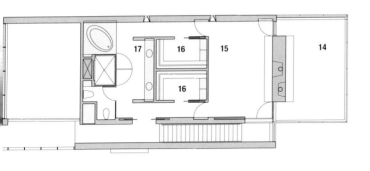

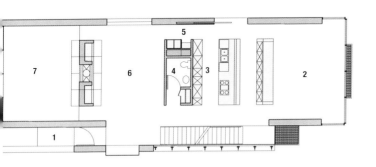

Palo Alto House

Palo Alto, California, USA
Swatt Architects

The owners brought to this project a passion for architecture, a wealth of ideas and a desire to create an artistic family home with unique materials and details. The result is a lively composition of dynamic spaces, rich materials and intricate detailing.

The design started with the concept of dividing the building program into two major wings: a 'public' and adult wing, and a guest and children's wing. A dramatic double-height central entrance gallery links the two wings and contains the principal horizontal and vertical circulation for the house. This gallery juxtaposes a cast-in-place concrete wall on the street side with a two-story glass curtain wall on the garden side. The curtain wall extends the interior spaces into the garden and provides visual links between the separate wings of the house. A steel-framed stair, clad in maple, floats between the walls of the gallery, folding around a glass wall suspended from a stainless steel cable support system.

A major theme of the house is light. By day, natural light enters the house from a number of dramatic sources. The garden side curtain wall bathes the public spaces of the house with light, a skylight over the glass bridge of the library sends a shaft of light into the living room below, and two large oculus skylights highlight the concrete wall of the gallery. At night, soft light from the interior makes the house glow like a lantern in the garden.

Vibrantly painted walls, unique light fixtures, modern furniture and an extensive collection of contemporary art complement the complex architectural composition.

Photography: Cesar Rubio

Portsea Beach House

Portsea, Victoria, Australia
BBP Architects

Set among hauntingly beautiful moonah trees, this luxurious resort-style beach house provides a cul-de-sac that emerges with dramatic moments.

The home has two extensive living areas, four bedrooms, a study, and numerous bathrooms including a luxurious ensuite opening to a private courtyard space with a private spa. Because of its size, the house was designed as two interlocking wings: one for the guests and children, the other including kitchen, dining and living, the main bedroom and parents' retreat and/or second living area. The brief also included a garage area to park three cars and a boat.

To minimize the 5380-square-foot (500-square-meter) footprint of the house, the basement garage level was wedged into the site, providing a solid base to support the northeast wing. This wing acts as a rectilinear capsule with a series of cubes infiltrating its clean exterior. The cube cut-outs articulate the views, balconies, and entrances. The rock wall provides a warm fabric to flank the secondary wedge, which then peels away to present the cantilevered wing. The clean parapet walls of the wedge hide a soaring light roof structure, lightly supported by a curtain of glass.

Horizontal spaces open panoramic views to the outside. To the rear of the building, the horizontality is heightened and further accentuated by the timber canopies and screens, and is only broken by the cut-outs inviting the user to weave between the built form and the landscape.

The deck area incorporates a large swimming pool, with an adjacent space that can either become part of the main deck area or be closed off by a pair of Japanese-style screens to become a private outdoor space to the master bedroom. The use of water is integral to the design of this house. Not only is it present in the location of the swimming pool, but also in the courtyard that intersects the two main wings of the house. An ornamental pond with continually moving water creates a contemplative feature to the living areas.

While the forms of the house are clearly modernist, the clean lines of the building have been softened by the selection of materials and colors. The house is primarily clad in timber and stone, selected to engage with the context and colors of the site.

LOUNGE

DINING

KITCHEN

DECK

SWIMMING POOL

POND

LIVING

SPA

MASTER BEDROOM

ENSUITE

W.I.R.

LAUNDRY

ENTRY

STAIRWELL

POWDER ROOM

STUDY

BEDROOM 3

BEDROOM 2

BATHROOM

BEDROOM 1

DECK

LAUNDRY

GARAGE

Steinhardt Residence

Birmingham, Michigan, USA
McIntosh Poris Associates

The program included a ground up, three-level house with two porches (one screened-in) and a private terrace. The first floor includes a living room, kitchen, dining area, 'keeping' room (sitting area near kitchen), and a powder room. The second floor includes the master bedroom, master bathroom, and a home office. On the basement level there are two guest bedrooms, a guest bathroom, and an exercise room.

This very contemporary house is set amongst more traditional homes from the 1920s. The initial concept was to build a loft as a single-family home. The result—an urban townhouse—is very open with minimal intervention in the space. Storage areas are either hidden or used as room dividers. As well, as an individual house, the clients get much more light than would normally

be available in a multi-tenant loft building. The steel-framed house has concrete floors with radiant heat (maple on the second floor), exposed metal deck, steel trusses, limestone fireplaces, soapstone counters, aluminum-framed commercial windows, and exterior simulated stone blocks. Sea wall—usually used on piers—is used for the retaining wall. The architects worked with the client (an interior designer) to integrate all the materials, interior finishes, and furnishings. Several levels are at play, with the master suite overlooking the living room, and a subterranean terrace, which the owner refers to as her "Soho terrace". Although the house is on a corner lot, with lots of windows, it still affords the owner a sense of privacy.

Photography: Balthazar Korab

Stone House

Chicago, Illinois, USA
Stuart Cohen & Julie Hacker

The house was built on a wide suburban lot that had never been built on before. The unique feature of the property was a number of large stands of mature trees. To preserve these the owners relinquished a rear lawn and the house was sited at the back of the site. This produced a driveway approach alongside a wooded yard. The house's exterior is clad entirely in a buff colored stone, with a cedar shingled roof and lime green colored casement windows and trim.

The main spaces of the house, along with a master suite, are on the main floor. The owner wanted a great room rather than separate living and dining rooms. These are visually combined into a single space with the two areas defined by changes in the direction of their beamed ceilings

and by a column screen. At the end of the living room is a fireplace with translucent French doors on either side. These open into a home office and the master bedroom, which are interconnected.

The owner has four sons who were soon to go off to college. Their bedrooms plus a shared study and lounge area comprise the second floor and are tucked under the roof, giving the house a lower profile. The boys share two identical interior bathrooms, which borrow natural light through transom windows from a skylight over the central hall. The stair to the second floor continues up into a tower room, which affords views of Lake Michigan one block away.

Photography: Jon Miller/Hedrich-Blessing

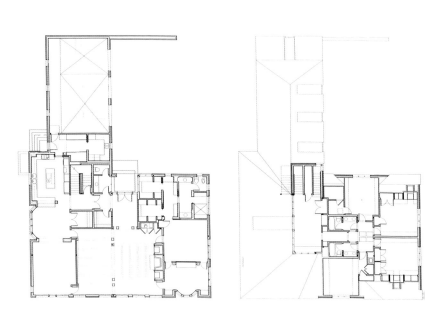

Swatt House

Lafayette, California, USA
Swatt Architects

This project is an architect's own home for a family of five including three young children in Lafayette, California (approximately 20–25 miles east of San Francisco). The residence is situated on a north-facing site, overlooking a creek, mature oak trees, and the hills of Briones Regional Park beyond. The design takes advantage of the rural views to the north, while maximizing natural daylight from the south. Exterior spaces, including a swimming pool, two terraces, and a south-facing entry courtyard, have been designed to promote a strong connection to the natural environment.

The interior of this house is organized around a glazed, south-facing, two-story spine, which serves to reinforce circulation, admit maximum daylight, and provide access to the entry courtyard. Five bi-folding glass doors open the spine and living areas to the entry courtyard, virtually eliminating the separation between indoor and outdoor space.

The internal organization of the house is expressed on the exterior by material changes. Horizontal cedar board siding and mitered glass enclose the spine and contrast with the integral colored stucco skin of the main living spaces. In form, the house is quiet, restrained and modern, building on the language of earlier modern West Coast architecture.

Photography: Russell Abraham, JD Peterson, Indira Jivandran

The Old Dairy

London, UK
Thomas de Cruz Architects/Designers

When the owners bought this former dairy, set among the 19th-century residential terraces of south London, it had already been converted into a house. However the rear courtyard and collection of outbuildings remained ramshackle and undeveloped. The owners, who had considered moving to Sydney, were inspired by houses overlooking Sydney Harbour and chose to work with London-based architect Peter Thomas de Cruz whose practice draws on subtropical design influences to breathe light and life into the stuffy English housing stock.

The traditional Victorian frontage belies the fact that the house has been completely remodeled in a contemporary manner. The existing staircase filled the hallway, cutting the house in two. By removing the staircase and locating a new one to one side of the hallway, the architects were able to free up space and create a new vista from the front door right through to the end of the rear courtyard garden. Bright light, even on the grayest London days, now draws you through the hallway and into a spacious living/dining/kitchen space that spans the full width of the house. To create the living space, a large extension has been inserted between the side access from the street and an original two-story rear addition. By removing all visible means of supporting the existing addition and the original rear wall of the house, the rear ground floor of the existing house has been seamlessly connected to the new extension to form one coherent space.

Drawing on a response to subtropical climate for inspiration, the house has been opened up to the rear courtyard across almost its whole width, with folding/sliding doors, an overhanging canopy roof and a level floor finish that blurs the division between inside and outside. The zinc-finished extension roof is pitched upward, away from the building to draw light and views of the surroundings and sky into the living space. Using tall glazing and rooflights, the previously dark, cellular layout has been liberated by an outward-looking aspect and an abundance of natural light.

The outward-looking theme of the ground floor has been carried through to the second-floor level, where a large loft space has been converted and extended to create a master bedroom suite with the feeling of a penthouse apartment. Making the most of the low-scale nature of the city, folding/sliding doors, a frameless glass balustrade and rooflights generate a sense of space by providing views over the neighboring rooftops.

Photographer: Andy Cavill

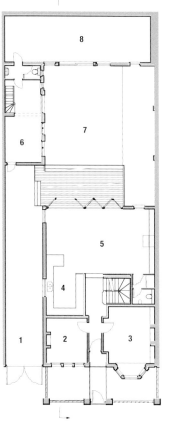

1 Entrance hall
2 Study
3 Reception
4 Kitchen
5 Living/dining room
6 Studio/office
7 Garden
8 Family room

Trahan Ranch

Wimberley, Texas, USA
Tighe Architecture

The 3200-square-foot (297-square-meter) project is situated on a 14-acre (5.7 hectare) sloped site with native oaks, natural springs, and unobstructed views. The layout of the house is a direct response to the site conditions and includes a 260-degree panoramic view. The buildings are nestled into the brow of the hill and have an unassuming appearance from afar.

A series of contradictions are explored through the architecture, including heavy and light, front and back, open and closed, and the contemporary and the vernacular. The grounded front is made of heavy materials that rise from the earth and is in sharp contrast to the more ephemeral back. The structure rises and becomes lighter at the down-slope side of the house as it opens to the landscape. The main house is a contemporary interpretation of Texas Hill Country post-and-beam construction that makes use of regional materials and the abilities of the local tradespeople. The spaces of the main house flow from one to the other with no doors while the guest room appendage has a more traditional layout.

The design includes a hydronically heated concrete slab on grade. The concrete foundation and walls provide high thermal mass. Large overhangs and covered walkways offer protection from the sun and cross ventilation is used. Natural materials are used throughout including concrete,

steel, stone, and metals. Texas Hill Country limestone was picked from the site and used to create the oversized Rumford fireplace that is central to the living space. An arbor connects building components and is an armature for solar photovoltaic panels that provide power for the property. The landscape consists of regional drought-tolerant plants that are native to the area and the local ecosystem.

The steel frame structure is a kit of parts that was prefabricated in a shop and erected on site. The steel pieces attach to a series of exposed board formed reinforced concrete pylons that are a vertical extension of the foundation. A storefront aluminum glazing system of laminated opaque glass fills in the surfaces between the concrete piers and makes up the exterior walls. Exposed steel beams cantilever out from the concrete pylons and support the tilted roof plane. Steel pipe columns, splayed at unexpected angles, buttress the structure outside of the building footprint.

Photography: Art Gray

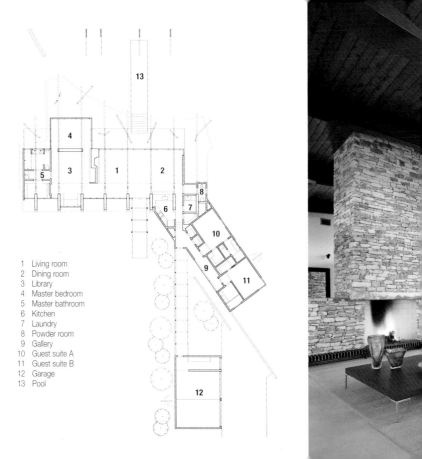

1 Living room
2 Dining room
3 Library
4 Master bedroom
5 Master bathroom
6 Kitchen
7 Laundry
8 Powder room
9 Gallery
10 Guest suite A
11 Guest suite B
12 Garage
13 Pool

Webster Residence

Venice, California, USA
Steven Ehrlich Architects

Located in Venice, California, the Webster Residence utilizes the oasis of an interior courtyard as an antidote to the urban context. Just a half-block from the beach, the rectangular lot fronts a pedestrian street, one of only a handful of streets closed to traffic in Venice. In plan, the building consists of two volumes at each end of the lot, linked by a service spine on the east and the central courtyard complete with a reflecting pool. Moment frame steel I-beams frame roll-up glass doors on the two façades that face the courtyard and the front façade that links to the street. This open axis provides an unparalleled level of open space, with an uninterrupted flow from the ground floor living and dining in the front across the courtyard, and up a flight of steps into a rear studio through another roll-up door. The amphitheater-like steps that rise from the courtyard further enhance this procession of space. The raised platform not only provides an additional vantage to enjoy the exterior, but it also moderates the site's 5-foot (1.5-meter) rise in grade from front to back to allow for a two-car garage at the alley. When all three garage doors are opened, the house transforms itself into a pavilion of connected courts and spaces.

The layout of the house introduces several upper-level terraces and a large roof deck to allow the owner private and public venues to enjoy the views of the Pacific. The general feeling of the house is of complete openness, but with sliding curtains, spaces are transformed into private hideaways largely concealed from public view. The glass roll-up doors on the lower level allow spaces to flow uninterrupted into the exterior, expanding the livable area of the house without constructing additional square footage. The courtyard spaces moderate the warm summer temperatures and provide a comfortable micro-climate through lush plantings and running water. Additionally, normally enclosed rooms such as the bedrooms and studio are opened to the outdoors in a matter of seconds with oversized roll-away windows mounted on the exterior façades, and aluminum-framed sliding doors.

Constant ocean breezes allow for natural ventilation to the point that the house has no air conditioning system. A central heating system was included but is only necessary on the coldest of nights, particularly with the thermal mass provided by the concrete floors.

Photography: tideworks Benny Chan

Williers House

Tampa, Florida, USA
John Howey & Associates

Situated on an in-town wooded lot for a bachelor whose place of business is nearby, this residence was designed with two zones in mind: a public zone, entered from under a bridge to a central two-story living space edged by glass, to a courtyard-enclosed pool with views of surrounding oak trees. At one side is the formal dining room, kitchen, bar, and garage. At the other side is a guest bedroom wing. The personal sleeping-recreation zone is situated above the master bedroom, with a dressing and bath wing with a nautilus-inspired shower for two. This zone is connected by the bridge to a large recreation space with a hot tub and exercise equipment at the other end.

Because the residence is located on a corner lot, and to save a large existing oak tree, the structure was turned 45 degrees to its site boundaries. All zoned spaces focus out, with large glass areas, balconies and decks, to the private wall-enclosed landscaped swimming area. Formal entry is to the gallery bordering the living space with a circular stair from the gallery to the second-level balcony. All spaces have high bands of continuous glass to provide uninterrupted private views to the many oak trees and natural landscaping.

Photography: Steven Brooke, George Cott

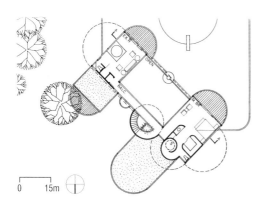

Windy Hill

Northern Mississippi, USA
Ken Tate Architect

Stretching for miles across the property, a gated private road winds from the edge of one of Mississippi's small towns. Turning onto the driveway beyond the big gates, prairie gives way to extensive gardens, and a Norman manor house is revealed. The house looks as old as the mountains. Indeed, its rough stonework consists only of weathered rock, from the face of a mountain. Constructed over five years, the whole seems to have evolved over centuries, as did Norman residences on both sides of the English Channel.

Landscape architect René Fransen's plan drew Tate's architecture out into the countryside. Axes extend in all directions, punctuated by structures of Tate's design. Tate imbued the dovecote, pump houses, tractor shed, greenhouse, and poolhouse with the elegance that the French bring to the most utilitarian structures. The poolhouse terminates one end of the pool's axis, and faces the pool's arched and fountain-fed grotto. Ending the axis of the croquet lawn, a late renaissance exedra doubles as a garden seat, for gazing toward a newly created private lake. Off the rose garden, in what seems to be the dovecote, is the grandchildren's multi-story playhouse. Off its own cour d'honneur, the wood-paneled garage is but a preface to the wonders of the interiors beyond.

Inside, the Tates have marshaled their design teams in creating what at first seems to have grown by haphazard accretion, but then reveals itself to be an interior firmly grounded in classical ordering principles. Charme Tate contributed her own nuances to the process. In came flooring from a demolished chateau, and silk draperies hand-painted in London for the job. Antique tasseled passementerie adorns drapery surrounding a painted Portuguese bed. The longroom, breakfast room and stair hall have woodwork that was made in England, from re-milled antique heartwood. The woodwork's makers traveled to Mississippi, to install their paneling and niches, and to apply an authentic limed finish. Particularly brilliant among Ken Tate's moments here are things such as the box-bay, with its rough-hewn timbers and leaded glass windows, juxtaposed against the very formal French drawing room. Then, there is the brick-infilled half-timbering off one wing, and all the perfectly reproduced details that reveal the acute skill embodied in the Normans' joinery methods.

Photography: Gordon Beall, Richard Felber

Wood Residence

Hillsborough, California, USA
House + House Architects
Brukoff Design Associates Inc.

In an affluent community south of San Francisco, this new home recedes into the center of its site, nestled into its south-facing slope. By a simple rotation, the house turns blank walls to the neighboring homes and opens wide to protected views. A detached three-car garage is connected to the house by a covered breezeway through a quiet garden with a sloping stone wall and a beautiful Japanese maple tree. A gray slate walkway leads to the front door past birch trees and a curving black steel fence. The crisp form of the house is achieved by the use of tightly spaced vertical wood siding and integrally colored stucco that layer the forms against one another in varying shades of taupe.

The living, dining, kitchen, study, powder and master suite are located on the main floor with wide expanses of glass to the views. Modulated ceiling shapes give definition and division between spaces that are open and flow together. Rooms spill out onto a large curving wood deck with glass panel railings that disappear against the view. At the lower floor, the family room, guest bedrooms, laundry and workshop are reached by a curving stairway with tall windows to a broad, protected view into the gardens.

The front door is fabricated in maple, cherry, ebony and stainless steel with flanking panels of sandblasted glass. A cylindrical cherry column frames the passage into the vaulted living/dining area where warm maple paneling on the ceiling glows. Cherry cabinetry and granite counters at the wet bar continue into the kitchen and in the powder room where they become sculpted art pieces. With windows on three sides, the kitchen and its adjacent seating area are bathed in natural light.

Photography: Tom Rider

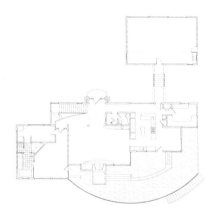

Woods Drive Residence

Los Angeles, California, USA
Aleks Istanbullu Architects

The clients called for more contiguous living space in their home, while maintaining the exterior. The site is a hilltop with spectacular views of Los Angeles from downtown to the ocean. The existing house, built in the early 1990s, was essentially a 6800-square-foot (632-square-meter) white box with black windows.

The architect reorganized and renovated the interior of the home around the light and views at the site, and the need for a showplace for antiques and contemporary art. Some walls were removed, and the dining room ceiling was raised. The space was actually reduced for better flow of space. A curved exterior wall transects the building, and leads one to the cherry wood front door. The interior portion of the curved wall has insets and niches to provide nooks for sculpture and other art. The wall is faced with ochre-colored acrylic plaster on one side, and teak paneling on the other.

The passage through the interior starts narrowly and then pans out to reveal the view. A broad living room is filled with fine antique furniture placed in conversational vignettes accented by antique Oriental rugs. A decorative wall with elaborate green damask upholstery and an ornate mirror provides a transition between the space for antiques and the rest of the contemporary interior.

Much of the first floor is organized around a two-story, light-filled central staircase court. Light from the stairway skylights and windows increases natural light throughout the home, particularly in the kitchen. The kitchen itself was completed, renovated, and faced in cherry wood with marble counters. Like the large living room, the bedroom is a broad expanse of open space punctuated by carefully chosen furniture. The large master bath sports marble counters and plenty of storage behind cherry cabinetry. A small vanity area was carved out of a niche between bathroom and closet.

1 Entry
2 Den
3 Bathroom 3
4 Living room
5 Dining room
6 Breakfast room
7 Bedroom 1
8 Stair
9 Closet
10 Bathroom 1
11 Broom closet
12 Kitchen
13 Storage 1
14 Pantry
15 HVAC room
16 Bathroom 2
17 Garage

283

INDEX

Index of Architects